Baseball Coloring Book for Kids

This book belongs to:

_____

© **Copyright 2021 – All right reserved**

You may not reproduce, duplicate or send the contents of this book without direct written permission from the author. You cannot hereby despite any circumstance blame the publisher or hold him or her to legal responsibility for any reparation, compensation, or monetary forfeiture owing to the information included herein, either in a direct or an indirect way.

Legal notice: This book has copyright protection. You can use the book for personal purpose. You should not sale, use, alter, distribute quote, take excerpts, or paraphrase in part or whole material contained in this book without obtaining the permission of the author first.

Disclaimer notice: you must take note that the information in this document is for casual reading and entertainment purposes only. We have made every attempt to provide accurate up to date and reliable information. We do not express or imply guaranties of any kind. The persons who read admit that the writer is not occupied in giving legal, financial, medical or other advice. We put this book content by sourcing various places.

Please consult a licensed professional before you try any technique shown in this book. By going through this document, the booklover comes to an agreement that under no situation is the author accountable for any forfeiture, direct or indirect, which they may incur because of the use ofmaterial contained in this document, including, but not limited to – errors,omissions or inaccuracies.

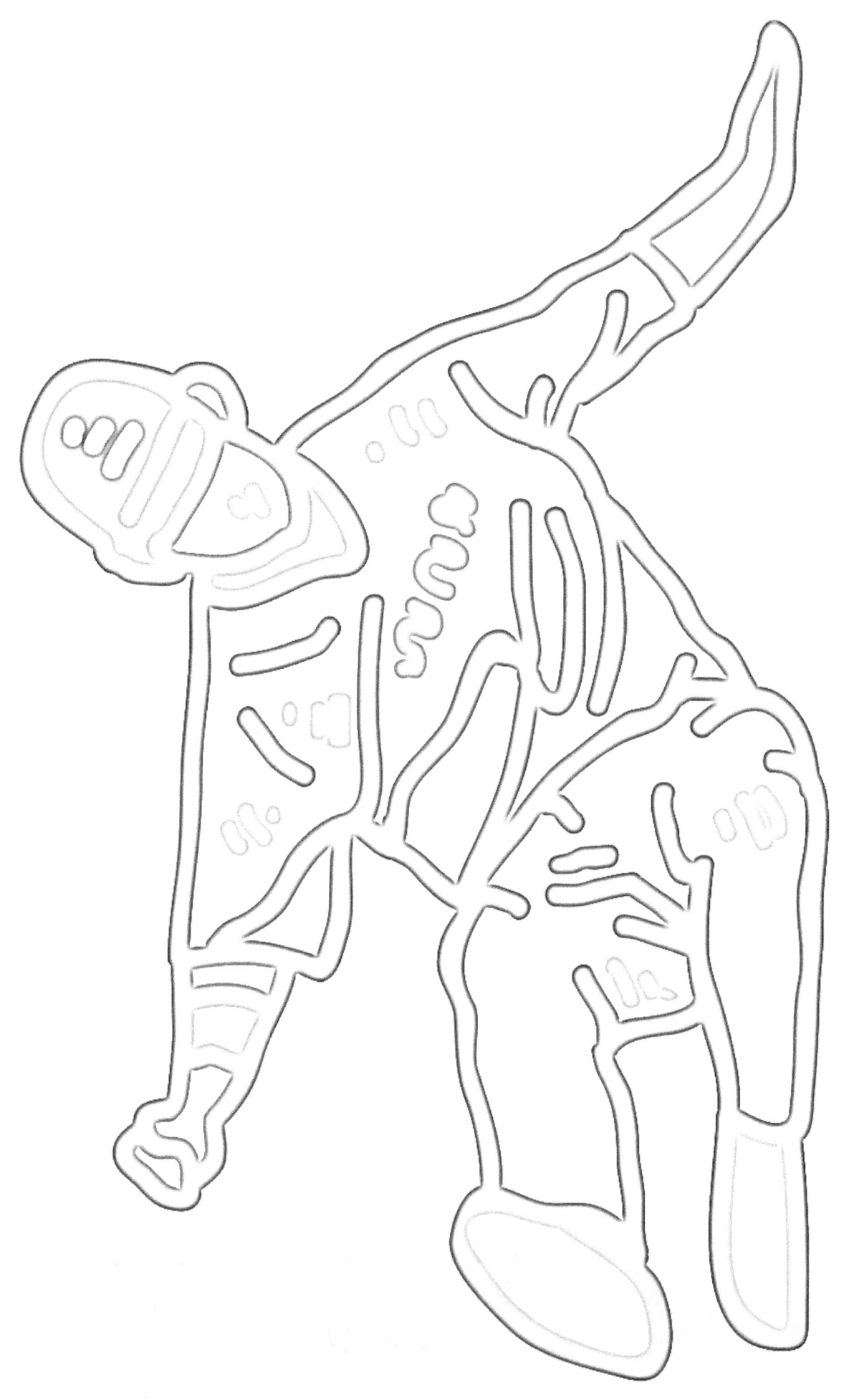

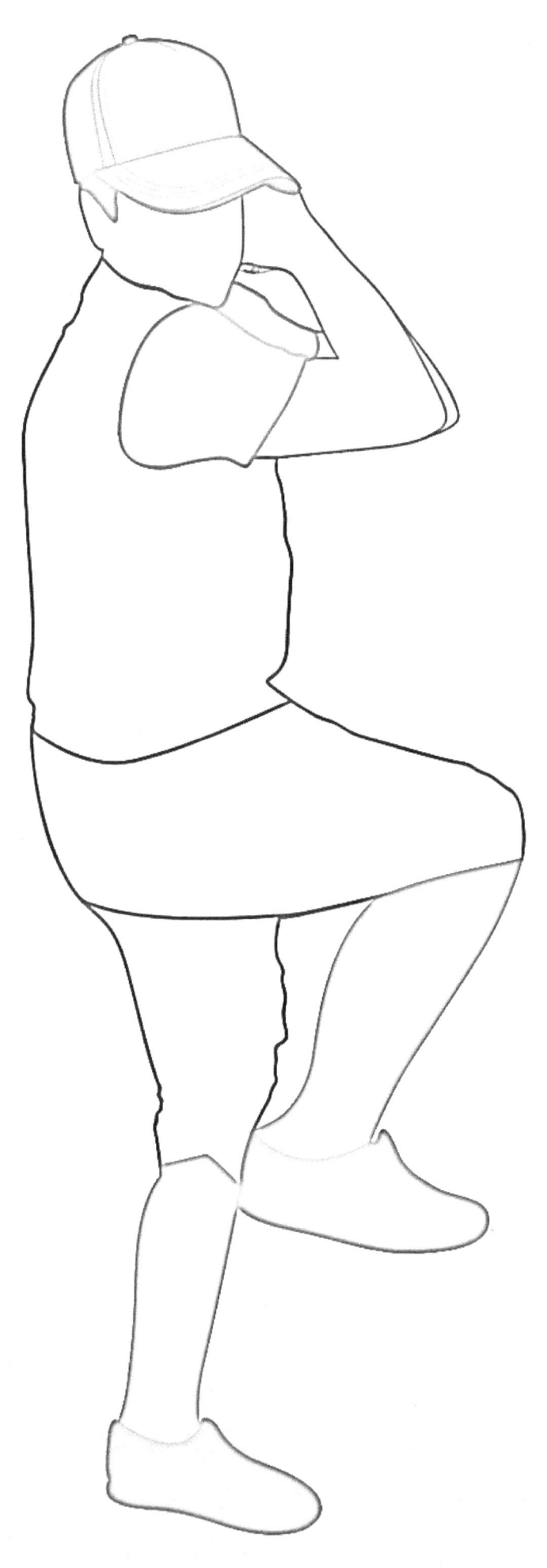

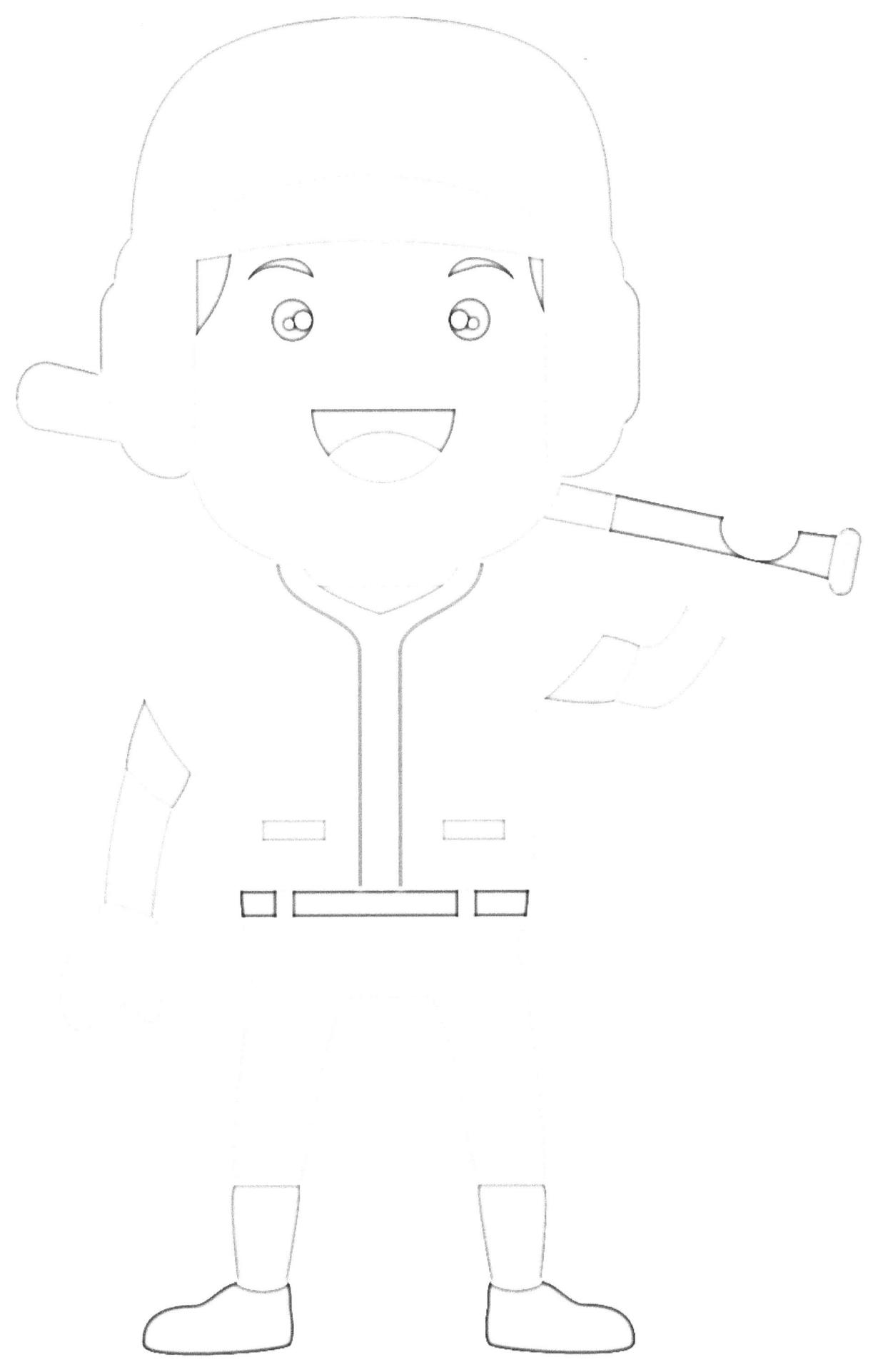

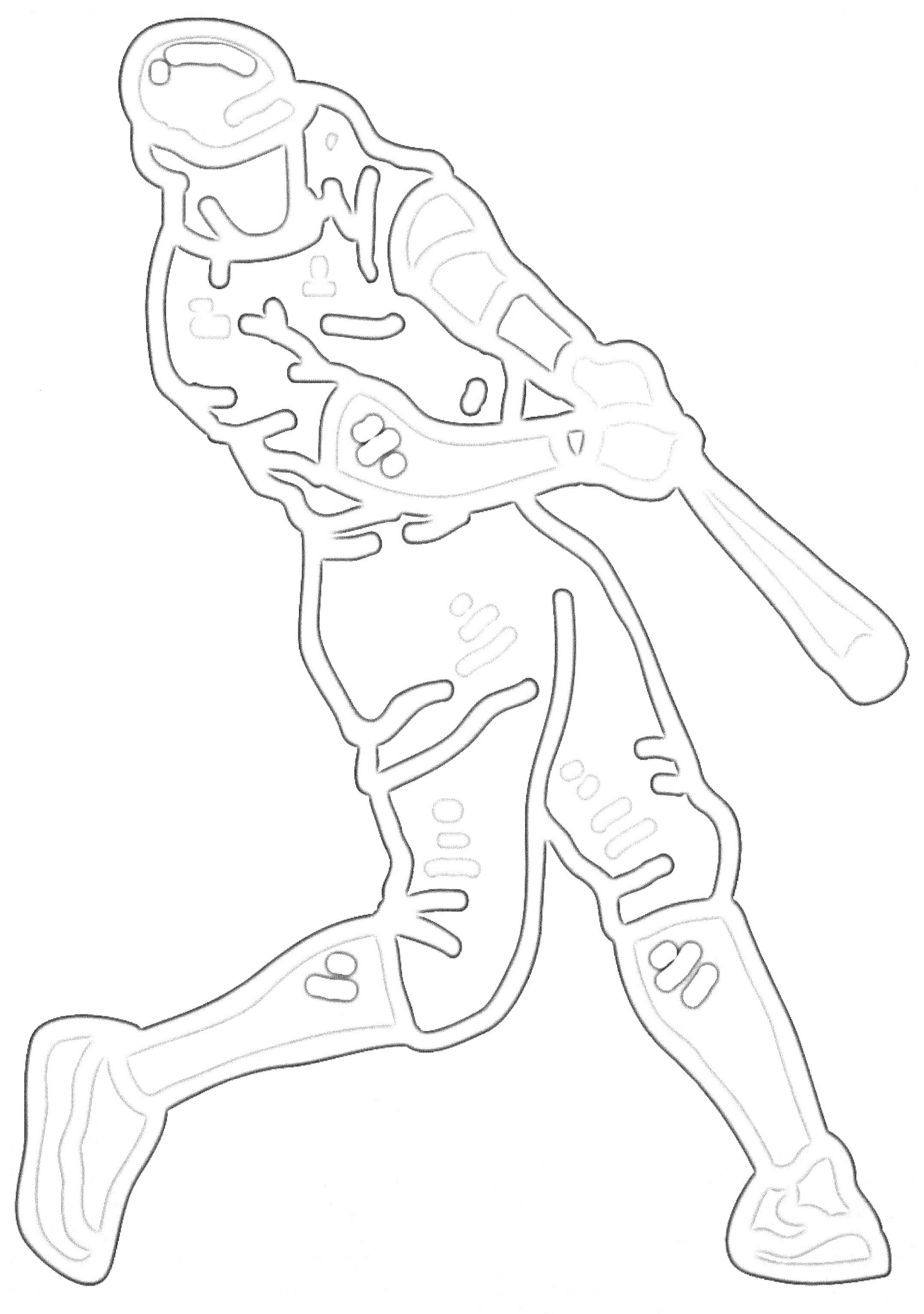

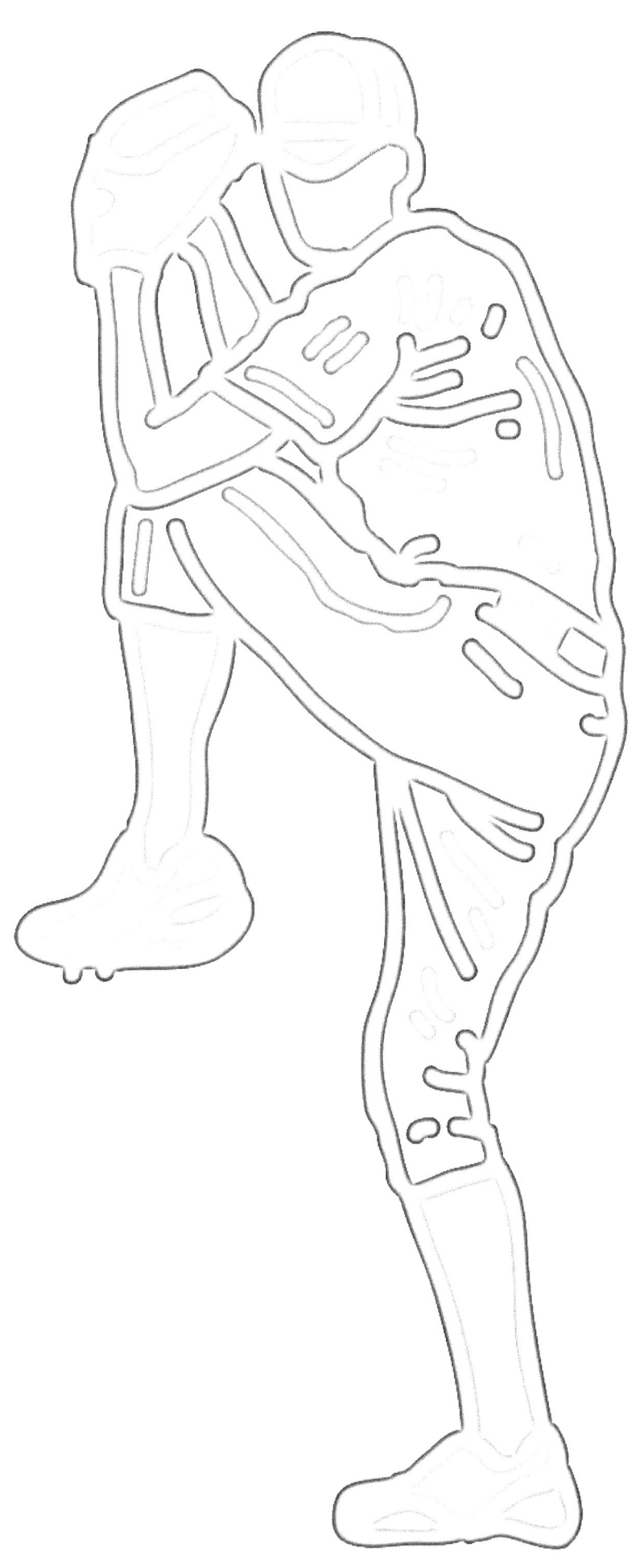

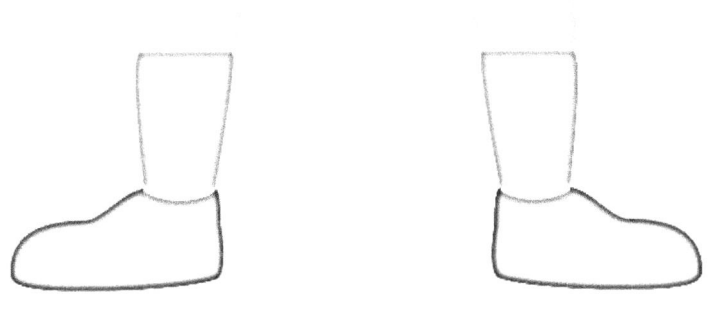

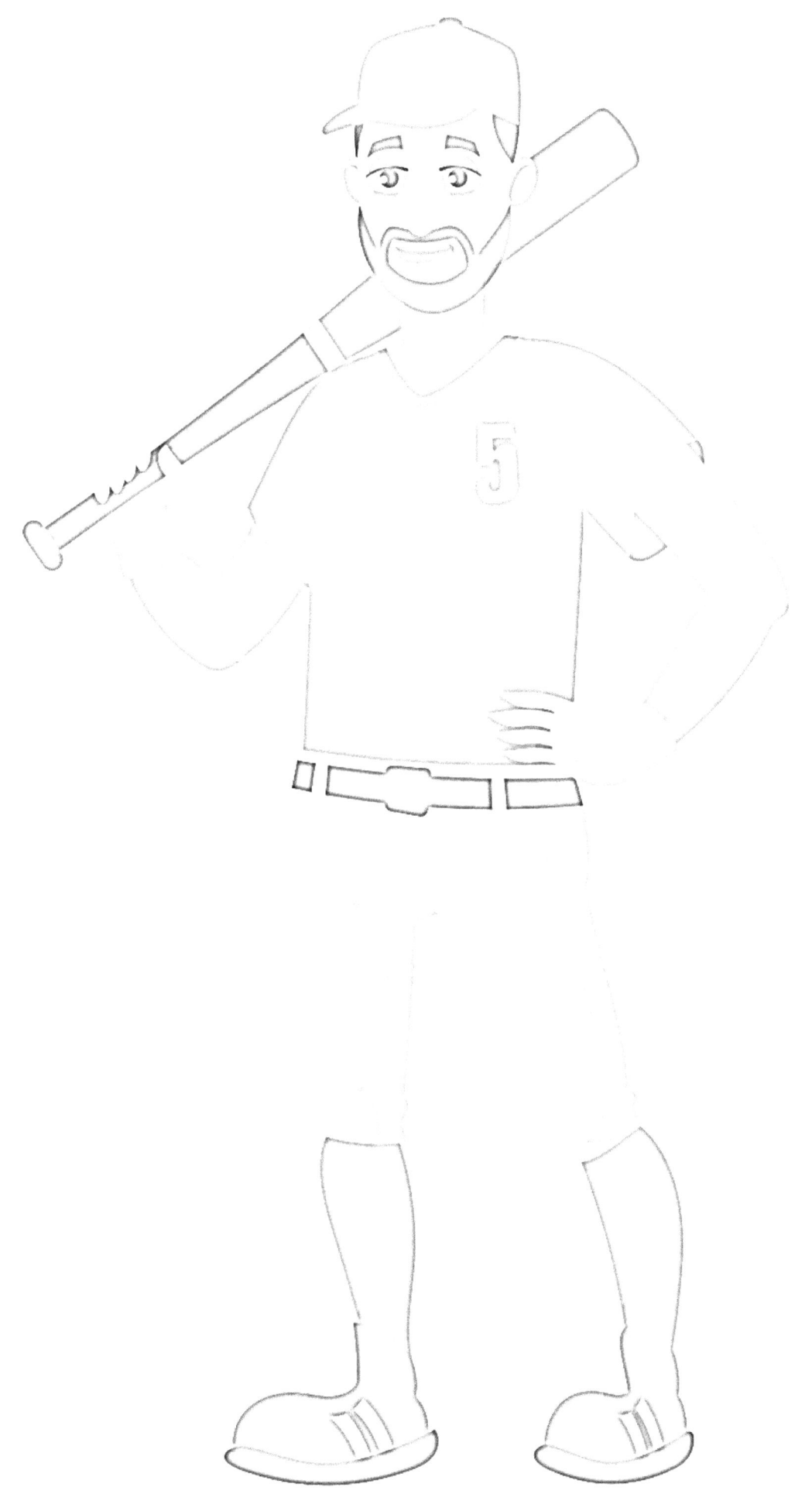

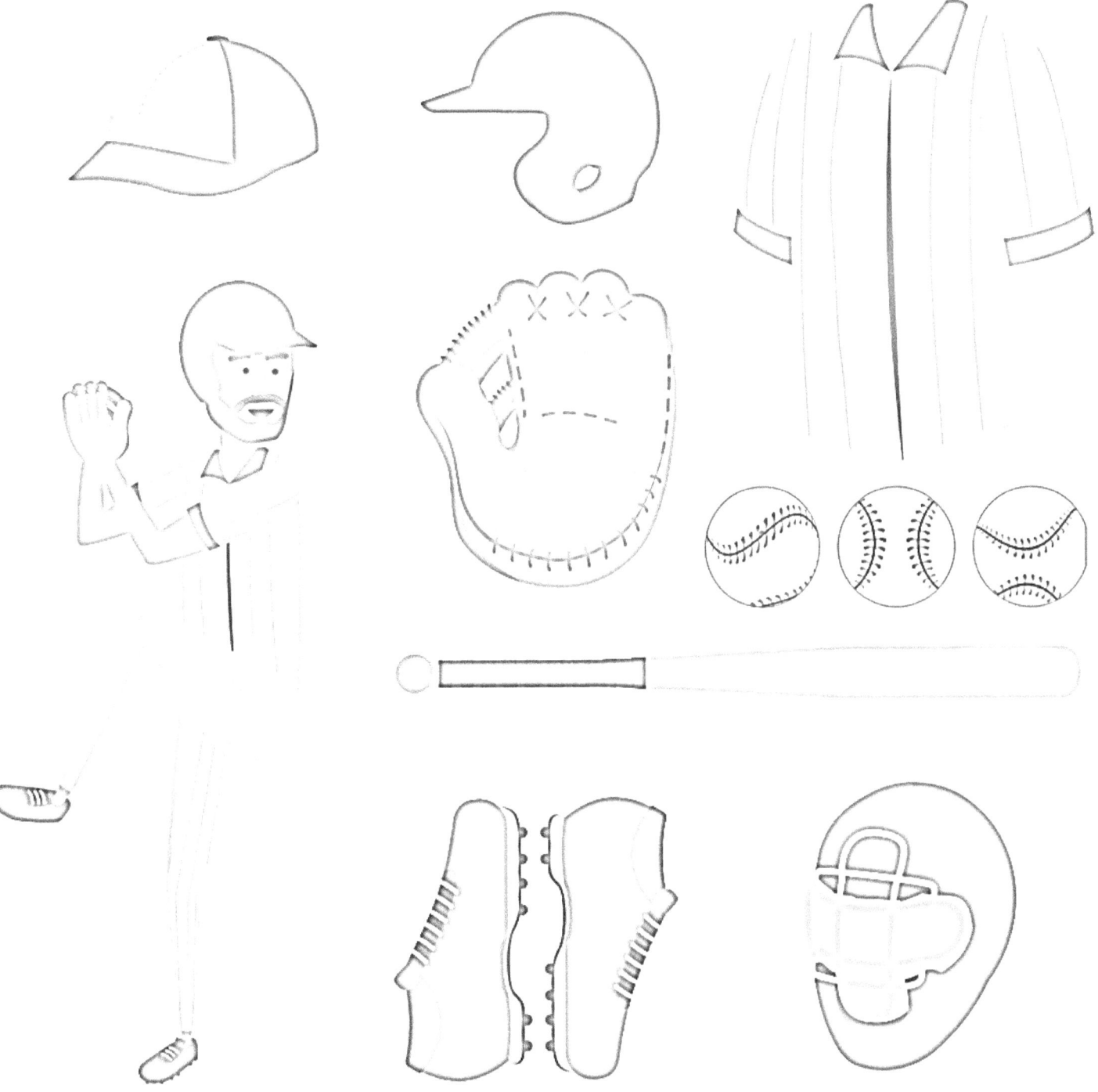

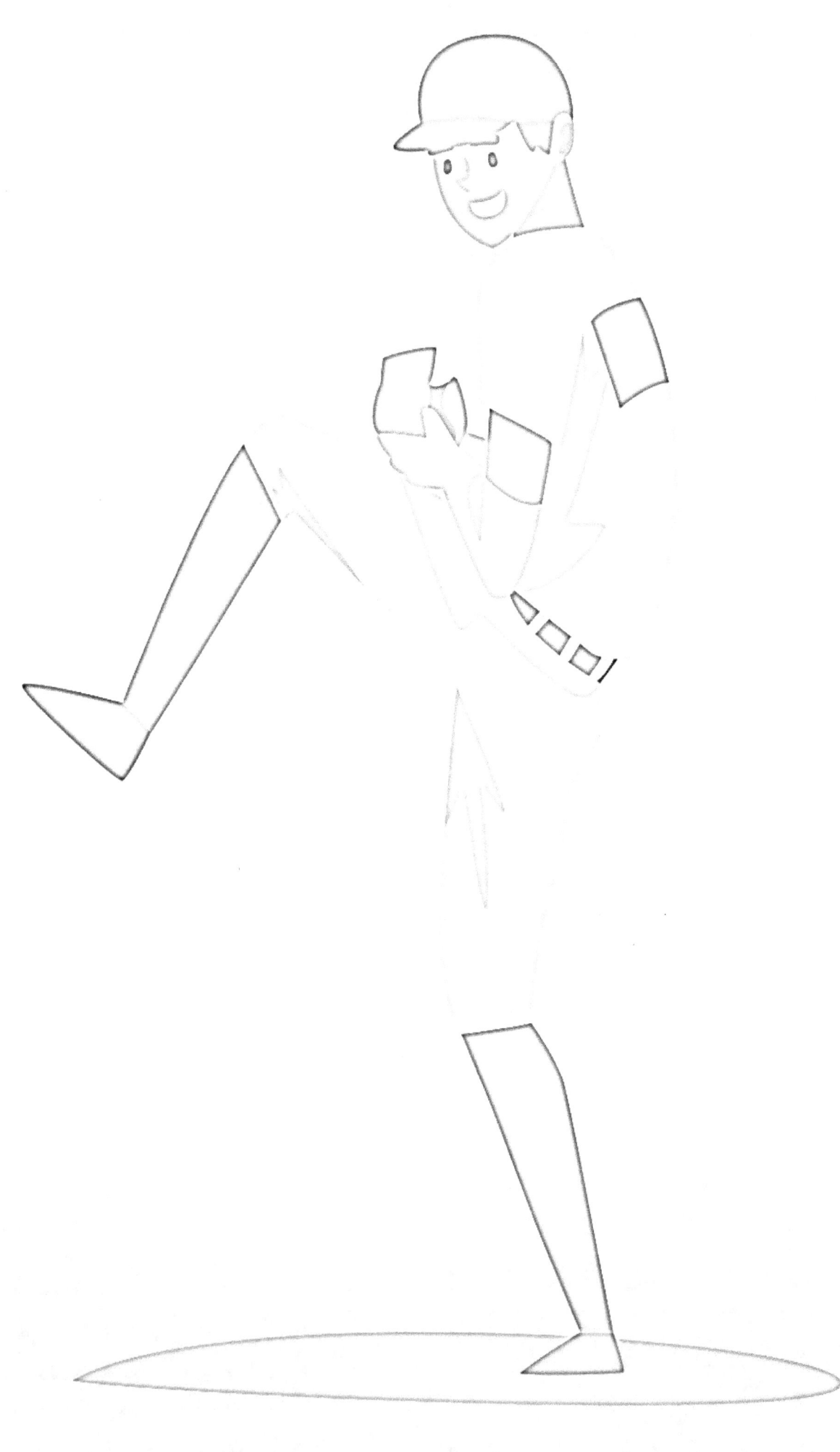

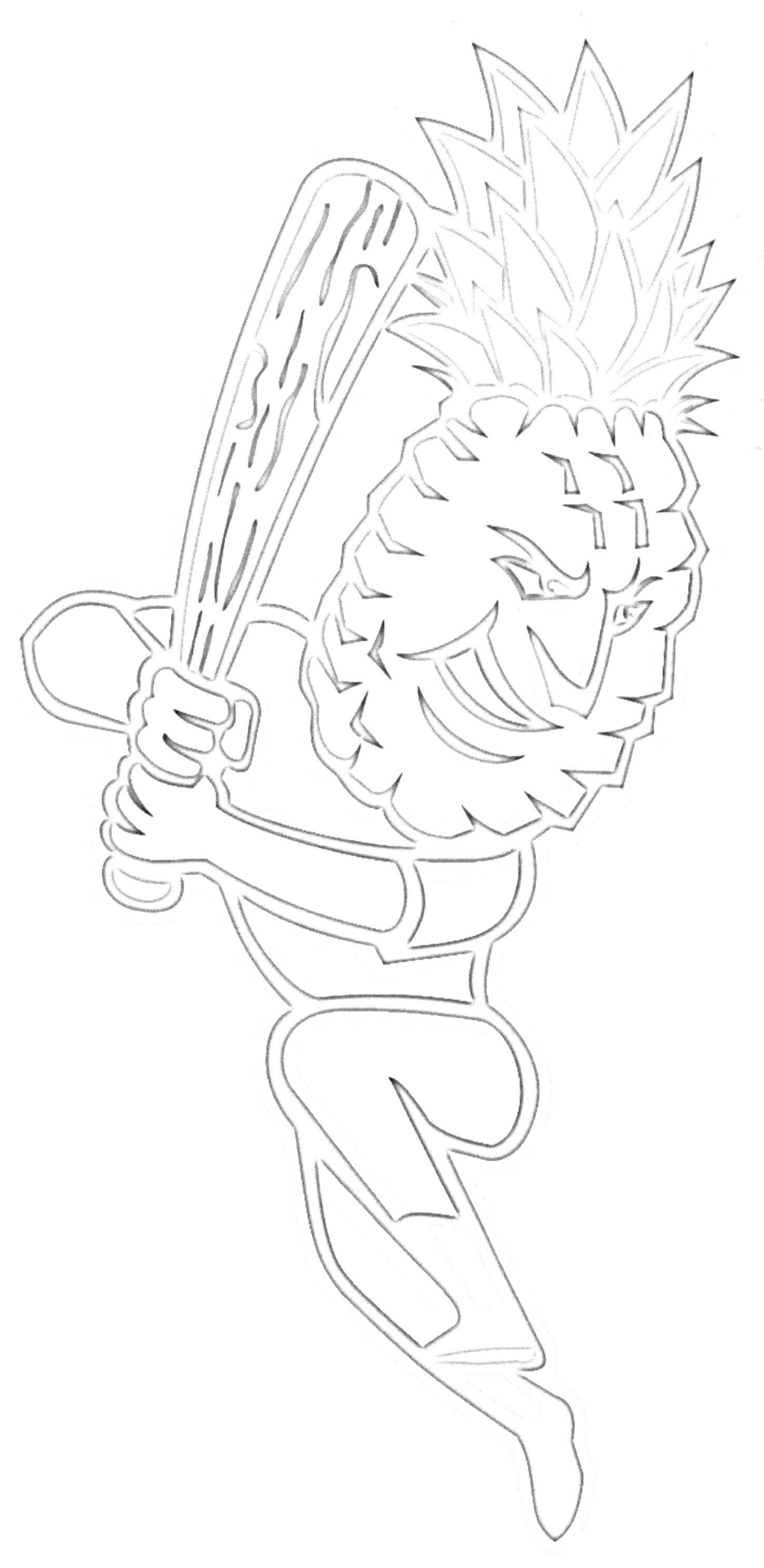

Thank you!

We hope you enjoyed our book!

As a small family company, your feedback is very important for us.

Please let us know how you like our book at:

office.babeljoy@gmail.com

www.ingramcontent.com/pod-product-compliance
Lightning Source LLC
LaVergne TN
LVHW060215080526
838202LV00052B/4278